WESTMINSTER WEST

TUPELO PRESS
North Adams, Massachusetts

WESTMINSTER WEST

POEMS

Chard deNiord

Westminster West
Copyright © 2025 Chard deNiord
All rights reserved.

ISBN: 978-1-961209-23-7 (PAPER)
978-1-961209-42-8 (EBOOK)
LIBRARY OF CONGRESS CONTROL NUMBER: 2025932263

Cataloging in Publication record available on request.

Tupelo Press
P.O. BOX 1767, NORTH ADAMS,
MASSACHUSETTS 01247
(413) 664–9611 / editor@tupelopress.org
www.tupelopress.org

Tupelo Press is an award-winning independent literary press that
publishes fine fiction, nonfiction, and poetry in books that are a joy
to hold as well as read. Tupelo Press is a registered 501(c)(3) nonprofit
organization, and we rely on public support to carry out our mission of
publishing extraordinary work that may be outside the realm of the large
commercial publishers. Financial donations are welcome and are
tax deductible.

COVER ART:
Liz Hawkes deNiord, "On the Edge of Sky." Acrylic, 30 x 30 in.
Used by permission of the artist.

Cover and text design by Dede Cummings

ACKNOWLEDGEMENTS

Paris Review: "Tablet"

Antioch Review: "Héloïse To Abelard (October 3, 1115)"

American Poetry Review: "Second Paradise"

Plume: "The Widow at Point Reyes," "The Other," "The Book of Guests" "Bronchoscopy," "Odysseus To Calypso, A Dead Letter," "Skywriting Over The Rockies," "The Shame," "Rerun"

On The Seawall: "April 9th, 1965, Appomattox"

The Massachusetts Review: "This Side Of You"

Green Mountains Review: "Like Wax," "Abelard To Héloïse (July 15, 1115)," "Héloïse To Abelard (September 21, 11115)," "Abelard To Héloïse (September 27, 1115)"

AGNI: "The Lake"

Poetry Porch: "Adam's Lament," "Eve's Lament"

Ashville Poetry Review: "Night Nurse"

American Poetry Journal: "Weather Woman," "What Holds Them Together," "Mallard"

Tupelo Quarterly: "In The Beginning"

Dreaming Awake: New Contemporary Prose Poetry From the United States, Australia and the United Kingdom: "How To Teach Poetry To Freshmen," "Lizard, An Exegesis As Love Letter," "This Was The Test"

Vox Populi: "Love In The Time Of Covid," "Turning 70," "Grief Is The River With A Foreign Name," "Songbirds Fly North At Night"

Greensboro Review: "Credo"

Rustica: "Westminster West, Vermont, June 20, 8:03 PM"

Brighton Press and The Poetry Porch: "Adam's Lament" and "Eve's Lament"

American Poetry Review: "Second Paradise"

On The Seawall: "Late Work In Early Winter"

Body: "The Myth Of Virginia"

"Dispatch From Gaia" and "I Stand Beneath The Mountain With An Illiterate Heart" were commissioned by the organizers of The Feverish World Symposium that took place at the University of Vermont in 2018 (https://ecoculturelab.net/feverish-world-symposium)

CONTENTS

I

II

III

I

THE WIDOW AT POINT REYES

She sat for an hour watching 10,000 tiny silver fish
swimming around in Abbotts Lagoon, talking
to the dunes, calling their bluff, reading every-
thing that came to mind into the clouds that floated
by above like cosmic erasers.

How smug and doomed
she felt, but also wise, which seemed ridiculous
if true at the time in the way truth feels
when it's gone too long without a nod
to the hieroglyphs in the sky.

The tiny fish
swam like checks in every direction they turned.
What was she to think other than they approved;
other than they were so many silver yeses
to whatever she was thinking, no matter how strange
or *wrong*.

Down at the shore, giant waves descended
onto the beach in rhythmic roars.

She told
the body of a rotten mackerel picked clean
by gulls the word.

"Can you guess my sweet,
my love?" she asked.

"I'll give you a clue.
It rhymes with you but can't be spoken or heard."

TABLET

If the King of Uruk had never wrestled Enkidu,
the wild man of the steppe, and just barely defeated him
on points, he never would have fallen in love with him
with a love that was greater than that for a woman,
nor asked him to go hunting with him in the Sacred Forest
for the monster guardian, Humbaba, the beginning
of history as an ageless story would never have happened.

If the king had never suffered the loss of himself
in another, he never would have known himself
as someone less than himself without his beloved,
nor hurt with a grief that rendered him listless,
although he called his suffering "nothing" with a smile
to the face of the Queen of Heaven who craved
his devotion but couldn't have it—his only solace
for being human.   If he hadn't grieved so deeply,
he never would have grown into the comedian he did,
nor swum to the bottom of the Sacred River to pick
the flower that the shaman said would bless him forever,
nor almost drowned while diving for that blossom
with a godlike breath, nor tasted the salt in the river
that cursed him with a thirst for wine and hatred
of mirrors, nor mastered the art of curling his tongue

around the diphthong in death, nor learned
how to say the single sound of *e, a,* and *u*
at the center of beauty, nor loosened his grip
on the thorny flower as he slept on the beach

oblivious of the snake traversing his body
then hissing to the darkness "only I am eternal,"
nor dreamed of grilling a gazelle stewed in garlic,
then eating it with his wife and children
in a joyous reunion at the marble table
in his hyacinth garden.
                              If he had never slept
so deeply, he would have felt the serpent absconding
with his flower into the forest where she devoured
it whole, then shed her skin, he never would have made
his way back home with his grief for his friend,
nor gained the knowledge of how to read the text
of clouds as one long sentence that spelled his end,
nor discovered the secret of how to string
the smallest things together as he spent the rest
of his life ruling his kingdom, building a wall around
his city, telling stories to his brilliant children, planting
his garden throughout the morning, happy with his title
Comedian King, lying in his hammock, dreaming
and waking, waking and dreaming.

ODYSSEUS TO CALYPSO, A DEAD LETTER

I lived with you on Ogygia
like a jar fly with catchy timbals.
I was the voice in your mirror each morning and night.
I was your "angel" with a heart that didn't sleep.
You said, "Sometimes we burn so clean nothing's left."
You said, "Love isn't enough."
The leaves were falling.
Everything smelled like falling leaves.
I didn't believe you.

HOW THIRSTY

The earth is yours and everything in it.
ANONYMOUS

How thirsty I grew from being satisfied.
The same sugar that rose
from the earth rose also in me.
I planted myself on a bank.
Masqueraded as a willow.
Wept with joy above the river.
Wept with sorrow above the river.
This was the still ritual for feet—
to know the earth like a root.
To imagine my body as a tree.
My tears were clear, both sweet and bitter.
One leaf cried out to another,
"Empty me today of all my color.
Fill me tomorrow with a shot of sugar."

THE OTHER

You must believe without
any evidence or reason
to believe that your beloved
is standing behind you waiting
for you to turn around by ro-
tating only a little at first
and then some more until
you see her face and smell
his hair that emanates a scent
that's a lot like yours, only
better, then feel the tickle
of her breath on your lips
and cheeks and hear his
voice that speaks your name
with an accent you've never
heard before but are drawn
to for its inflections and music,
although you're still afraid
to turn completely around
and regard her there as your
beloved who appears so
stunning you find it hard
to believe he's actually there
and wonder if maybe she's
a ghost or vision, although
he seems so real and alive
with lilac breath and
riveted stare you can

feel the charge of her skin
through his dress that causes
you, in turn, to believe against
every reason and fear in the
mystery that compels you to
keep turning around until
you behold her form and
visage so completely it con-
tinues to beguile you each
time you blink and become
so dizzy you can't stop
staring at him as the cynosure
who stands at the center
of your turning, which causes
you next to grow oblivious
to everything else because
you've met her now in
the flesh and can think
of nothing else besides him
in this danger zone of turning
around which causes you in
yet another turn a close call
with oncoming traffic and
loss of appetite and for-
getfulness, which you only
survive at the mercy of
a god who's employed by
another god whose name
you're forbidden to speak,
although the animals repeat it

in the wild, until in the midst
of your obsession with her
you find yourself in private

with him in a room some-
where beside a river with
the exigent need to make
an exchange from you to her
in the paradox of the transitory
realm of eternal being in
which you walk away
together into the world
that's been transformed
by only your turning
around to behold your
other so you could walk
away transfigured into a
field like gods remember-
ing that moment you first
beheld each other in your
raiment of everyday clothes
and embraced as one, al-
though you were two and
so vastly different you could
never have known from
seeing his face that she was
the one, if you're ever to love.

ADAM'S LAMENT

You came the last but were the first to learn
that coming last, you were the first in turn,
a second thought of God's and dream of mine.
I understand the curse of your position.
I too would pray for an obvious sign.
My loyalty softens as my faith conditions.
You were blessed with cause; I can't object.
I understand your wanting back my dream.
Your bitter syllogism is correct:
I am a man and thus not what I seem:
the only child for whom my children grieve.
I have vivified them too from dream,
but they unborn and yet to be conceived,
came only after we had been deceived.

EVE'S LAMENT

I am granted a few last words by the oak
that only listens: a few vain wishes
and cigarette I refuse to smoke.
I wish my husband, the minor poet of fishes
and trees, had seen the world with greater vision,
had stopped to hear the ocean's legion
of silent names. See how he ribbons
the trees, as if they were endangered women.
See how he stares at what's forbidden:
each flower and fruit, each orange and lemon.
Why listen to a man who polishes his tongue.
Who never took time to listen to the koan
of crashes when he wasn't present? I am on
my way to a country that can't be sung.

HÉLOÏSE TO ABELARD
(MAY 19, 1115)

> *And if the name of wife appears more sacred and more valid, sweeter to me is ever the word friend, or, if you be not ashamed, concubine or whore.*

HÉLOÏSE

Read your planctus, brother, so I can log it in my niche.
Make soft the marble floor on which the spirit springs,
then sing to the friars who sleep in the yard: "I'm besotted
with an angel who reads both Latin and Greek."
Exegete the dark of my circumference on the altar's slab
where you drink and eat, then forgive me if you can.
Hold forth in your pulpit, darling, then preach
your *Sic et Non* all night. Cross yourself with nothing on
as you repeat: This is my body, love, take, write, conceive
our little Astrolabe.

ABELARD TO HÉLOÏSE
(JULY 15, 1115)

You swam like a snake with your head upraised.
I cut a wake inside your wake until you stopped
and stood in the mud.
                              I held you in a tight embrace
as if you'd break on letting go.
                              I saw the sky
for what it was: immaculate field, burial ground.
A voice cried out from across the lake: "Abelard!
Héloïse!"—your uncle Fulbert calling us to return
"right now!"
                    A thousand minnows circled our legs
like shiny badges.
                          I couldn't speak as I gazed
at you too deep in bliss to utter a word, too damn ecstatic.
We swam ashore and dressed in vain.

HÉLOÏSE TO ABELARD
(SEPTEMBER 21, 1115)

You woke me to a dream of waking
in which I approached you and sang your name.
When I listened again I heard the song
of you as me in the sound of your name,
as if I were saying it with a voice in my head
that you could also hear and I was listening
for us both, or you were, although it didn't matter
which since the song rose between us
as we stood in a meadow, both separate and together,
fully involved in musical flames that accompanied
our voices in crimson robes with holes
at their center that were also our mouths.

ABELARD TO HÉLOÏSE
(SEPTEMBER 27, 1115)

We were getting ready for bed when suddenly
a horse called out from the upper field.
"It's Estaban," you said. "I can tell by his voice."
You ran outside with an open palm, which lured him down,
then mounted him in a single leap, pressing your knees
against his sides, clenching his mane as you galloped past.
"Do you see?" you cried. "Do you hear?"
A breeze blew through the universe and then the grass.
Everything was blowing, the sky, the leaves, your hair.
I took down your dress from the laundry line
and held it to my face, smelled the flames inside the lace,
took off my clothes and put on your dress
as a new garment that gave me strength.
I saw that acts were the same as thoughts.
I saw unseen things in my dreams.
You made a joke of "yes and no" by singing it to Estaban
to the tune of a nursery rhyme.
You made me hard beneath your dress.

HÉLOÏSE TO ABELARD
(OCTOBER 3, 1115)

We lay on the bank of a beaver pond and stared
into the dark of the dammed up river, remember?
A hawk floated overhead as the sun went under
and a chill distilled the air. I felt eternal then
for just a moment in which nothing mattered
beyond my listening, although I can't remember
anything you said, only that we talked until dark
and a star came out, and then another.

ABELARD TO HÉLOÏSE
(OCTOBER 20, 1115)

This was the test: to see you in other things
without mistaking you for the things themselves
in equations that confused my friend, the scientist,
with sums that were *incorrect*, but true enough
despite their broken equal signs that hid the truth
in this ecstatic calculus: your belly is a desert
with hidden springs, your hair a cataract that falls
and stays, your thighs a current of mountain rivers,
your hips two dunes that fall and rise, your toes a school
of piccolini, your eyes two stars that shine as millions,
your smile a blade that sharpens itself, your lips a fig
that ripens on my mouth, your loins the valley
through which I pass.

LOVE IN THE TIME OF COVID

"He died alone, and he will be buried alone."
Der Spiegel

The darkness arrived without your voice
or touch and yet I heard your voice
and felt your hand in mine.
Nothing in the end, not even death,
can loose my grip from yours.
What can I say that echoes here
and beyond? Just this: you were always
so contagious, dear, my hazelnut, my vast,
but unlike this germ, you infected me
with a love that made me better
than well, that was a gift of bliss
I didn't deserve.
So take these words that are not mine
but the ones you gave me
in the silence of this room and I return.
You were there, I tell you,
you were there when I was crossing
from there to here,
and you are here as well, right now.
No absence, yours or mine,
can fill itself with itself anywhere
when two have loved
as we did love, if only for a time.

SKYWRITING OVER THE ROCKIES

"Oh, darling in the distance
who appears so near," I whisper
to the back of the chair in front
of me.
        All these trips on jumbo
jets you'd think I'd arrived by now
in the Eschaton.
           I float down
the aisle in my head and think
of the fuselage as the church
of everywhere at once in which
I'm both here and there, both awake
and asleep with prayer.
            I order
a glass of pinot noir, then close
my eyes and make oneiric leaps
in a dream of us in which we're flying
together like angels, which is why
I suffer the sudden delusion of thinking
I might already be living my afterlife
in a Cloud of Unknowing, never mind
the sudden turbulence and warning sign
to remain seated and buckled up.
"The eclipse of mente and corazón occurs
in the planisphere of our bed at home,"
I write with my trigger finger in the air
as if it were a page in the sky.

"I'm always so regretful in the clouds
because I think I should know more
that I do.
          "It's enough," I say
to myself, "to know I'm simply
burning, which is to say, imagining
a fire in which I sit like a stone
immune to the flames but aglow.
Alas, I'm ready as we descend
to test my theory of believing
in the music that plays in the silence
of the fields of Sharon, silent as it is
and soul-affrighting.
                    To lie with you
in a loft somewhere and cup
your breasts and smell your hair
and kiss your lips and close my eyes
and read the text inside my lids:
"Hear the voice of yourself
in the sky that speaks in analects
about how to fly on Earth."

THE SHAME

I sat in my chair on the porch rocking back
and forth in the August breeze when suddenly
the phone rang waking me from a dream,
flashing the name of an old friend with whom
I'd fallen out of touch decades ago
in the way old friends do without
meaning to. I said, "Hello, old friend,"
at which he echoed me and then, as if
no time had passed at all we started talking
in the way gerontians do, knowing that
"neither fear nor courage saves us."
We began by shortening the years into minutes
with news: our children and wives and careers
until my friend suddenly turned
in a non sequitur to the trip we took
in 1970 to the coast of Maine
when the war was on and neither of us had reported
for duty, deciding instead to disappear
on the lam until our car broke down somewhere,
forcing us then to hitch-hike home
with nothing to show for our crime except our grief
for friends who were dying for reasons no senator
could explain because there were no reasons,
and then the reason why he really called:
to see if I remembered that girl with nothing
on at Eggemoggin Reach, "Amphitrite"
he said. "Remember?" At which I said,

"Say again?" "Goddess of the Sea." "Oh, yes,"
I answered, "That girl on the cliff." "Yes,"
he said. "Then you do recall?" "Oh, yes," I said.
"How could I not?" "But you did, it seems."
"Only seems," I said. "I had to think
for a second was all. It was the shame I felt
and continue to feel for where we were on that acre
of heaven so far from the war." "We had stopped
at a cul-de-sac, remember, and walked for a mile
or so until we came to her on a ledge
preparing to dive from high above, then did:
a stunning swan into the swells where she
remained for over a minute before ascending
with a gasp and cried, "Your turn!" At which
we pretended not to hear and walked
away back to the car like the *boys* that we still were.

MALLARD

I regarded my love from across the river
as she painted spectral letters, and because
I had created *a unique distance from isolation*
on my side of the river, I regarded myself
as invisible in her ignorance of me.
Without thinking about the meaning
of her colors, I read them as a message
only I could read, then humbled myself
before a duck paddling down the river.
"Oh, lovely mallard, quacking cypher,
spectral sensei," I said to the creature.
"What can I say to her about the beauty
of her letters?" "That that ultramarine,"
he quacked, "and bright vermillion
are the colors of heaven inside you."

IN THE BEGINNING

We lived in bed, no matter where we went
or what we did; we were always there, pulling
the sheets up over our heads like souls
for whom bodies are gowns that weigh too much,
pressing ourselves so close to each other we felt
our skin cross over to bone. How many days
did we dream like this in our high stone room
to which we'd flown on the wings of little deaths?
We slept awake and woke asleep in a fire
we couldn't put out; in a fire that burned
from the inside out. What did we know without
saying? That we would suffer the weight we lost
without even trying when we returned, then walk
like turtles on the beach? How fast do you think we said
"Yes! Yes!" to the poor first god
when he asked us twice in separate rooms,
"Are you sure about this?" So fast, I can tell you,
that the birds outside our broken window thought
we were singing a song only they remembered.

NIGHT NURSE

She sits at the table in the lower lounge
writing reports, solving puzzles, keeping watch
while the patients sleep or try to sleep
down the hall to her left and right
in the hum of the turned down lights
that some believe are hidden cameras
for the way they flash and the clanging pipes
a secret code when the heat comes on.
It isn't what she does so much in the way
of work, hardly anything at all, in fact,
but the watch she keeps in the semi-dark
listening for the faintest stir or cry
from behind the doors that she keeps cracked.
She's the hierophant of *the floor* in whom
the patients place their trust to tell
their dreams and *voices* when they emerge
like ghosts from behind their doors
in the middle of the night because she listens,
listens for as long as it takes for them to believe
that they've been heard and also believed
before she leads them back to their rooms
and tucks them in with yet another "good
night." She knows she's a little crazy, too,
but never tells them this, whispering lines
instead to herself as someone else
on the stage of the ward, an actress
who plays the part in a play that never ends—
lines that tell the truth in a way that turns
the prose of *DSM* to poetry:

What is madness but the nobility
of the soul at odds with circumstance?

I am the self-consumer of my woes.

I am mad north-northwest. When
the wind is Southerly, I know a hawk
from a handsaw.

"How thin the line that can't be drawn
between the real and *real* like a thread
in the hem of a dress that's come undone
from the stress of merely wearing," she wrote
one night in the chart she kept on herself.
A handsome man broke her heart
her first night on the job—a lovesick
physicist whose beloved had "left him,
just left," he said, causing him, in turn,
to reify her in his mind like the cat
in Schrödinger's Box. "So she is every-
where at once, although I need the box
as well for holding her among the stars
whose shiny yeses echo in the hills
where David claimed his music 'went out'
despite the fact there was 'no music'
like God Himself, by which he meant
the apophatic fact of the holy "super-
imposition" Einstein proved was true.
True! So there in the hills the harp
and lyre and flute are real if silent, too,
to those who are deaf to them

with perfect hearing. Can you hear it
too? Please say you do." To which
she replied with a lie she felt compelled
to tell since she had also lost a beloved
as well not long ago. "I do. I do," she said,
although she never told the doctors this,
aware that they suspected it anyway
when reading between the lines of her
reports just how she felt and that nothing
they said or did could change her mind
about her art of hearing the truth in code,
then writing it down as the wildest fictions
the patients need for telling their *truth*
in the wake of their breaks the doctors call
"precipitating events" when taking down
their names, ages, race, and presenting complaints.

II

LIZARD, AN EXEGESIS AS LOVE LETTER

"I crept out of your dream in a phallic suit, then climbed the tree I called Do Not Eat! So when you woke, there I was in my Sunday best as a funny little guy with a complex tongue and stunted legs who spoke the double truth. I lived inside your head where I hissed, 'For every hex there is a blessing.' I doubled as Lord and Lizard, instilling dreams in you and then My most ironic gift: a curse, which in My love for you I also chose to suffer by sacrificing My legs and eating dirt. I reified Myself to wake you up in a form that belies the myth of our first talk. How could I be Myself for even a second if I didn't also suffer? Every creature inspires another in Me until so many exist I can't remember why or how they got their beauty from the way they hurt on Earth. But you, dear heart, were the wand I hid as a rib for waving My last most human trick. This was the risk I took. Forgive Me for the side effects. I had no choice beyond his need for you, your slow but gorgeous hunk. Beauty was never so innocent as when he awoke to find you there. This is the tale in only orthodox terms. I was that lonely in paradise when I had legs."

HOW TO TEACH POETRY TO FRESHMEN

Say poetry happens when words fall for each other like randy teenagers on a hot summer night in one of their father's pickup trucks in which, before you can say F-150 or Tacoma or Silverado, they start flirting and then kissing and feeling each other up under a full moon beside a placid lake down a dirt road and then rhyming and caesuring and eliding and anaphoring and alliterating and ass-onating and diphthonging and consonating and parataxing and leaping and syncopating and enjambing and then ending in a couplet of sound and sense that sings in the dark without any immediate or overbearing need for meaning that's nonetheless there which is how you can tell it's poetry in the final breaths of its little deaths when it's over.

SECOND PARADISE

Poetry is a dream made in the presence of reason.

ADAM ZAGAJEWSKI

I went for a walk with a girl I hardly knew
when I was a boy on a trail by a river
for a film I didn't know was being made
by a director I couldn't see or hear
behind his hidden camera in the clouds
and trees as we recited our lines
unwittingly with no idea of the plot
or ending as we walked for miles
in that paradise of a park, which is why
we were killing it on that cerulean day
in a way that was more real than the trail
itself, which has been razed, I've heard,
for a housing development, which means
the world in which we live today
has become an illusion since we both
still walk that trail where we were born
a second time in a paradise we walk
to this day in our heads, although
it's no longer there, despite the fact it seems
more real than when we were there
enchanted with each other, striking
our tongues against our teeth to light
the tinder between our legs and ears
and then our hearts that needed proof
of fire in the air as we walked like ghosts

until we were lost in a grove beside
the trail and lay down somewhere
we could never find our way back to
and made love on a bed of moss
despite our fear; where we were eternalized
in the film which we continue to screen
as a non sequitur in quotidian moments,
like right now on the patio where we
balance our dinners on our knees
and divine the darkness behind
our eyes to dream awake of that time
we disappeared into a vast which plays
on the screen that hangs from a cloud
on which our short that is so long
is projected in color one day and black
and white the next, transcending time
in the way it did that day on our walk
beside a river in which we witnessed
enough of heaven's fire in its water
to weld our memory of that ecstatic walk
to a vision that would last in the grass
of days we called forever, although
we are deluded by the film that has
no credits for the sake of heaven
and witnesses in its showings to the irony
of a metaphysics that surrenders love
and even the river to sweet oblivion.

*Housatonic: Schaghticoke for *the place beyond the mountain*.

THE BOOK OF GUESTS

They gamboled toward me in the field—two lambs
so happy to see me they lay down at my feet and sang.
"Where's your mistress?" I asked. "Where is she?"
At which they gazed up at me and said,
"In the field, master. Don't you see?"
I searched the field until I saw you running
toward me through the grass that whispered
a riddle in its chorus of blades:
"So short no matter how long."
And then you were there like a vision before me.
I sang "la terre nous aimait un peu je me souviens"
to a tune from the war.

Procne and Philomena.

Dumuzi and Inanna. Boris and Olga.

A train rumbled in the distance and its whistle pierced the air.

Maybe there were trains before the world
that we're only hearing now.

And everything else on rails and wings and wires.

You touched my forehead and said, "Remember!"
I smelled the lilacs then inside your skin, the roses
inside your breath, the sea between your legs,
the pears inside your breasts, the fire inside your head.
"You're all the animals plus one," I said, then kissed

your neck, at which your lambs leapt up
and licked my face. "Where is your mistress?" I asked
them again to make them laugh, which they did.

You've made a myth. Very good.
Let's return to the beginning for fun.
Call me one and then another: eland, catamount, falcon...
How many do you remember?
More and more the more I remember.

Touch me again on the lips this time.

But then you'll dream and forget.

But I remember when I dream.

Like what?

Like the time when time was hidden
and you were the gorgeous spy who slept
with me in the steppe, then shaved my body
and sweetened it with perfume, which frightened
the animals away from me for good.

And then?

And then I awoke and there you were.
You had survived my sleep to sleep with me again.
Like a book at evening, beautiful and untrue.

Like a book on waking, beautiful and true.

We needed the animals to see beyond ourselves.
To know no creature we might imagine
could ever be more strange or real than the ones
that roam the Earth already.

Best to admit we're fools for falling in love
each time we wake at the start of the world.

I think we can think and love, don't you?

I do, even now I'm thinking without thinking
that the speed of light within a vacuum is the same
no matter what speed we travel as mere observers
between here and there, there and here.

And I would say: listen to the grouse
keeping his beat in the distance,
which to say, refrain from going on and on beyond
the facts or that which is enough already.

So what would you write in *The Book of Guests*
for our host to read?

How about this, some thoughts I didn't think:
"This field in which we slept last night rose up
like a cloud and comforted us. Thank you.
We'd love to return next fall in late September

and then again in April the year after that, and so on forever."
Now you do better—a word or two on my back will do
with an applicator—a blue tattoo which bleeds
each time I read your lines in the river's mirror.

If I can, my dear. It's up to the lambs.
Bite down on this when I begin.
"The ashes on which we stand in the grass
are the eons the sun published as smoke.
Behold the lambs that leap and joke.
'Behold the music in the valleys and hills,
although there is no speech, nor are there words.'"

Enough, my love. Our blood and ink are one

RERUN

in which the moment of her leaving keeps playing
in the theater of your heart as the final scene
in the film called *Her And Me* zooms in
on you both at the top of a Grand Central stair
with her weeping for reasons you couldn't know
at the time but do now as you recall
just how sublime the ancient city was
and infinite, too, while your heart floods with loss
so full it floats your memory of her still
in the same recurring short of your and her
good-bye on the giant screen behind your eyes
in which you're standing together on the axis
mundi of a cold platform embracing and kissing
in the din of her train arriving from out of the tunnel's
oblivion into which it then returns with her
again and again in your sleep without a sound.

MEDEVAC

Off to the east above Monadnock, the speck
of a chopper between the clouds. I watched
from below like a child in my yard, knowing
in the time it would take to sharpen my saw
it would return with a victim inside. So, I prayed
as I waited for the thrum of its blades blending
the sky to a deeper blue on its return, and when
it did, I prayed again until the silence resumed
across the sky that was so vast I felt the hurt
of the person inside—a woman, I read the following
day; someone I knew, still hanging on.

TO THE MUSE

You woke me to a dream of waking
in which I approached you and sang
your name.
                    When I heard it again in the clouds
and river, I remembered the silence
in the sound of your name when you were here,
as if I were saying it with a voice in my head
that you could also hear and I was listening
for both of us, as you were, too,
and it didn't matter which since it spoke
all around us as we stood in a meadow,
both separate and together, fully involved
in musical flames that accompanied our voices
in crimson robes with holes at their center
that were also their mouths.

THIS SIDE OF YOU

Words are poor receipts for what time hath stole away.

JOHN CLARE

I think you're still here sometimes
calling to me like the thrush at dusk
inside the woods where I lose my way.
I search for you like a ghost myself
in all the usual places, stand on the shore
this side of you and speak to the river
that flows and stays, stays and flows.
Everything is deaf to what I say,
choosing only to speak in the single
tongue of its simple language: river,
sycamore, wind… I listen to the hills
and valleys with the hope that even
a breeze will cure my heart.
                              "Move on,"
it whispers in the honey locust abuzz
with bees.
          "Move on."
                         A few leaves
fall like empty pages.
                         I carry your stone
with a perfect ear for silence.

HECATE

stared at the sky from the seat beside him
as they lapped the miles on cruise, then woke
from her fugue at a stop sign in Bliss
to see just where they were and how
much gas was left. To turn from the sky
that sang to her and give him a kiss.

Back from their drive in the *Coupé de Ville,*
he dropped her off on Western Ave.,
then watched her float like a human cloud
down the street and into her house.

Earthly fool, lost chauffeur,
he searched for her down every road
for the rest of his life. Felt her cool,
chthonic lips on his in the dark
of every cruel, spectacular night.

THE PRIEST REPORTS HIS DREAM
TO HIS ANALYST WHO ADVISES HIM
TO RETURN HOME AND BE THANKFUL
FOR THE DEVILS WHO ENTER HIS DREAMS

"My wife is dancing with a lumberjack in the forest
at night in the light of the harvest moon, then lying
with him on a bed of leaves and moss.
                                          Each tree
I fell while regarding them shakes the earth.
I put down my Husqvarna beneath an elm
and walk back home where I discover her
then in bed with him upstairs, already
asleep.
I kneel beside her and whisper, 'You sweep
my heart like an oak sweeps the clouds from the sky.
The scent of your breath is like the sweetness
of phloem in the stump of a fresh-cut oak
and your breasts like two young does that feed
among the lilies.'
                        To which she replies in her sleep
'Love, my love, is the tree too large to cut.'"

THE MYTH OF VIRGINIA

I imagined the yard today as a copy of itself
from the day before—its only differences
so miniscule they'd be invisible if they weren't
so large in my imagined absence—the same
old gestures, twitches, and pauses of the birds
and squirrels on the branches of the maples
and birches, so close to where they'd been
just yesterday, but different now without a sign.
I stared at a sycamore whose leaves were flames
for the only reason I needed to know that they
consumed all things in the guise of leaves
and because I needed to keep the blue flame
blue that burns to the highest degree on the gas
of loss. I called it *nothing* with a hand above it
I couldn't see. There was a space at the table
for a child who's face I'd already seen.
Who had arrived with a smile in the shape
of a blade. I composed a psalm because
I longed to make up a story that wasn't true
but also was about a lovesick king who said,
*I'm poured out like water and all my bones are out
of joint; my heart is like wax.* Who turned
into a cardinal when he died and then
fell like an arrow through the sky,
turning as he fell into a drop of blood
that stained the earth of all Virginia.

PILLOW TALK

I swallowed the sun to keep it holy.
But there's a light somewhere.
It will disappear if you try to find it.
Then kiss me for a million years.
Dare I scorch you with my tongue?
Until I blaze like you!"
"Then what?"
"Shoot me dead."
"Again?"
"Forever and again if you would."
"Then lick my wound."
"I will. I am."
"A little to the left."
"And then...?"
"Nowhere!"

CLOUD-MAKING

I'm picking the corn
that calls to me from the garden
to dirty my hands in the Vermont dirt.
Pull the weeds.
The sight of you standing naked
among the stalks reminds me
of Enkidu's lover, no, Ishtar
in the clouds, no, Siduri at the bar.
"That's enough for tonight," you say.
"We can't eat all that."
Why is it that I always plant too much?
I walk over to you between the rows
of corn like the first man and grasp your hips
from behind, then kiss your neck.
"The earth is infinite," I say.
"How much is enough?"
A toad hops at your feet.
"I thought it was a rock," you say.
The clouds are empty pages I cannot read,
then can as they turn in the wind.
"The ground is insatiable," they say.
A hermit thrush yodels the password
for dusk as the earth rises up in us
like sap with the force of gravity in reverse.

III

BRONCHOSCOPY

My father wanted me to see
what he did for a living with the hope
that I'd grow up to do the same,
which was to operate on people
while they lay asleep in the dreamless
twilight of anesthesia. And then
one day when I was twelve he asked me
to peer into the lung of an elderly
man through a bronchial scope—
an engineer for the C&O Railroad
who had smoked a pack of camels
a day for forty years. We were in
an examining room of the hospital
in Clifton Forge, Virginia and I
was playing hooky in order to attend
my father's "medical school."
He asked me to step on a stool
he had placed beside the patient
seated below on a similar stool
as he held the scope like a sword
in both of his hands while looking
down the metal tube, and then
away. So I did without knowing
what to say except "okay."
"Now look down there like I
just did," he said, which I did
with one eye closed while spying
with the other the vast reticulate
labyrinth of speckled lung and

its sepia lining of pleura. The scope
was lit by a tiny bulb that pierced
the darkness of his insides—what I
would later come to call the *numen
saccus* when I had grown and come
to see the seat of breath as the
spirit's home—and the more
I looked the more that darkness
seemed to rise despite the light
at the end of the tube since I
was sure that I was seeing the end
of this man's life in the specter
of a shade that spread to my eye
like a presence I had never seen
before but recognized somehow
by its telltale umber and also the look
my father betrayed. It was then,
in only a moment of my gazing
away, that I saw in the beam
of the instrument's bulb the brilliant
lamp of a locomotive barreling
down on me along the James
with more than a hundred cars
full of coal with this psychopomp
at his window and controls waving
at me in the din of his engine and
cars on their hundreds of wheels
shaking the trees and sleepers,
shining the tracks in squeals,
and the whistle, too, that pierced
my ears as it rose to the clouds

where it disappeared into the sky's
cerulean blue, which was when
without any warning or my father's
signal, that the old man coughed
a ghastly cough, trembling as he did
from his shoulders down, propelling
a wad of phlegm into my eye.
My father chuckled like a god,
then gagged, "Welcome to medicine,
son," as I fell back into the arms
of the nurse behind me who said,
"You got an eyeful there, young man!"
then wiped it off—the holy sputum
my father reported the following
week, when word came back
from the lab, had tested positive
for cancer cells. But it remained—
that phlegm—as a film in my eye
that's thickened with age to a strong
clear lens for seeing straight through
the scope of time to the various, desultory,
inevitable ends of everyone I meet.

APRIL 9TH, 1965, APPOMATTOX

I attended the centennial ceremony
of the Civil War's armistice in Appo-
mattox, Virginia on April 9th, nineteen
sixty-five when I was twelve.
There were thousands of people there,
many of whom were digging up
Minié balls from the battlefield outside
of town, then selling them as souvenirs.
The grandsons of Grant and Lee were there
along with the Marine Band on a stage
festooned in red, white, and blue not far
from the courthouse where those generals
put an end to that most dread *American*
war.
          I lived not far away in Lynchburg
where my friends identified me as a "Yankee"
since I was born in the north and had lived there
for a while, which might as well have been a century
to them since that was where I was from.
We played "war"—a game in which the uni-
forms of my soldiers were Union blue and theirs
Confederate gray.
                    We re-enacted battles
in the way young boys do, especially
Gettysburg where more than fifty thousand
casualties occurred—not enough room
on our floor to accommodate that number
with our plastic troops, so we resurrected
the dead until we couldn't count anymore.

We "played" like this because of what so many
Southerners preferred to call that war,
which I will not repeat since calling it that
only serves to open its wound that's still
so thinly sealed and which our child's play
with plastic men both failed and succeeded in
burying it for a while, the horror and mayhem
of Vicksburg, Manassas, Antietam, Bull Run,
Shiloh, Chancellorsville, The Wilderness,
Cold Harbor, Gettysburg, the last
of which and bloodiest of all occurred
in early July, 1865
and which Abraham Lincoln on
his way to the site composed an address in only
fifteen minutes or so to those who were left
to observe the charnel ground: "We cannot ded-
icate, we cannot consecrate, we cannot
hallow this ground. The brave men, living
and dead, who struggled here, have consecrated
it far beyond our power to add
or detract. The world will little note nor long
remember what we say here, but it
can never forget what they did here."
It wasn't until that day in Appomattox
in 1965 when I observed
those scions of Grant and Lee on a makeshift stage
shaking hands as their grandfathers had
a hundred years ago that I felt the blood
in the dirt of that town and its surrounding fields
rise up in me like a flower and bloom in grief.

THE LAKE

He had already begun to cross over
and see things from the other side of his room.
He was already flying with invisible wings
in his chair, staring ahead as I wheeled him
down the hall. "Where would you like to go?"
I asked. "I'll take you anywhere."

                                            "Outside,"

he said, as if outside were everywhere
he'd ever been and wanted to return to
again and again. It was late April—warm
and clear. I rolled him out the door at the end
of the hall and into the sky. All winter long
he'd been breathing the same recycled air
inside his cinder block room, so even
though his senses were dull and his mind half gone,
he could smell the lilacs and hear the birds call out
to each other their various sexual, fricative songs.
"Shall we go for a swim?" he asked, gazing at the field
outside his room. He saw the lake on which he'd lived
instead of the field and wanted to go in. He saw
the sun shining on the rye as it waved in the breeze
to him to also wave. "Yes!" I said. "Yes!"
I struggled in vain to hold him down by the handles
of his chair, feeling him rise like a swing that wouldn't
come down, no matter how hard I pressed against
the ground. No no's anymore to anchor him here.
"Dive off the end," he said. "I'll follow you in."
To which I almost said yes again but refrained
this time because I couldn't find the tone

anymore to sound like the boy who had just jumped
in; because only he could see the veil
that lay before him as a lake expanding into
a sea I couldn't see but only hear
in the distance as its waves pounded the shore and then
receded beneath his chair into the vast
from which they came like hands and then returned.

THE LOGGERS

move from tree to
tree in the thrill of fel-
ling, feeling the sky in-
side their eyes as the
canopies open onto
forever and the blue blue
hue of heaven croons
a song called "nothing"
called "everything" as the
chorus of foliage soughs a-
long beneath the noise of
Brobdingnagian saws at
the necks of oaks, pines,
palmitos, kapoks, Bao-
bab, ashes, palms, ipé,
teaks, redwoods, lo-
custs, walnuts, mahog-
anies, birches, hick-
ories, beeches, cedars,
spruces, hemlocks, cher-
ries, and firs for a rea-
son they can't explain oth-
er than to say, "We're fol-
lowing a longing to
raze the trees we love and
because they're there is
all with a cost we can't re-
sist to tear the sky and al-
so—dare we say the supra-

lapsarian saw?—"be-
cause we can," which
sounds depraved, we
know, but echoes as a
call that lures us into the
oldest groves where the
hermit thrush incants a
song that grows as an aur-
al seed inside the ear in-
side our ears: "O holy holy
ah, purity purity, eeh,
sweetly sweetly" and the
chickadee's stutter up-
braids in vain: "There's some-
thing deeply wrong be-
neath that has swelled to
a progress that is no
less than the clear-
cut forests that are void
of any Hawthorne ef-
fect which might have dis-
abused you of the fact that
a tree amounts to on-
ly a stick on the scale of
your hearts when you've
felled so many you have no
notion of the loss you've
wrought because you've
thought from the start that
the genius of saws, skid-
ders, splitters, and trucks

permitted you license to
do as you wish which
you have, in fact, be-
cause it's your job—fel-
ling trees in heaven's the-
ater—and the industry de-
mands it and you're good
at it Goddamit and it's thril-
lling besides to watch
them fall so slowly a-
cross the sky and onto
the ground where they
shake the Earth itself like
the Word that fell at the
start and because the music
of cracks, crashes, and
thuds has drugged your
blood with a thirst to
drink the sky with your al-
ready loaded eyes in the
din of Husqvarnas, Poul-
ans, Stihls, and Tigercats."

WESTMINSTER WEST, VERMONT, JUNE 20TH, 8:03 PM

Often I am permitted to return to a meadow
as if it were a given property of the mind
that certain bounds hold against chaos.

ROBERT DUNCAN

I'm here in the meadow at dusk listening to the songs
of insects in the grass and birds in the trees that circle
the meadow—a chorus of voices I join in singing
with human songs that only silences them.
So many songs in one in their crooning to the sweet,
inscrutable darkness that falls like a curtain from oblivion
to the meadow, where it lands as a shadow that cools
the grass and leaves and stream that runs beside it
from off the mountain that looms like the shoulder
of a god who's dreaming dramas of weather that come true
throughout the year on the stage of the meadow
on which this multitude of creatures to which I'm listening
reprise their lyrics of wooing in the falling darkness
that stirs their hearts to calling out to each other
in the various fricative tunes they play on the instruments
of their legs and throats and wings until the darkness
deepens in the blessing of night and silences them.

I STAND BENEATH THE MOUNTAIN
WITH AN ILLITERATE HEART

We have to feel our own evolutionary roots and to know that
we belong to life in the same way that other animals do and the
plants and the stones...The real nature poem will not exclude
man and deal only with animals and plants and stones, but it
will reach the connection deeper than personality, a connection
that resembles the attachment one animal has for another.

GALWAY KINNELL

I stand beneath the mountain with an illiterate heart
and imagine the clouds as angels singing a silent song
that we can hear somehow because it's also echoing
inside us where a valley I call my "heart and mind
as one" listens and listens but never fully understands,
where my eyes also hear and hear from seeing
and seeing but never fully see. The Earth is crying.

I stand beneath the mountain with an illiterate heart
and listen to the hermit thrush I cannot see in the brush.
I call back to him in my human voice that makes
no sense beyond my hum. I believe in the power
of a song more than words to tell the truth in a musical code
that pierces the woods.

I stand beneath the mountain with an illiterate heart
and watch the animals and plants disappear.
They are being sucked through a hole in the sky.
I'm waiting to go. A year is a day.
The reel to reel is wailing.

I stand beneath the mountain with an illiterate heart
whose alphabet I can never know but only marvel at.

A voice cries out from the mountain's summit:
"Lie down again before the lords of Earth and let them creep
all over you. Let just one of them speak for all the others
the way they do." When I say I can't, she whispers back,
"You must. Just listen to the voice inside the song
of every animal, plant, and stone. It's the chorus
called beauty. It's the list we were born to keep adding to.
No one who fails to see himself in a fox or fly or ant
can speak for another, although his voice may boom
like thunder in a crowded hall, although he may charm
a throng with empty words, although he may think
the shadows are real on the wall."

I stand beneath the mountain with an illiterate heart
and squeak then howl in response to a toad
called golden, to a parakeet called Carolina,
to a tiger called Tasmanian.
"Each letter of Earth is so inscrutable I know
I'm living forever when I behold them.
I must do what I must to save them.
Today is tomorrow.

DISPATCH FROM GAIA

*The question of landing somewhere did not occur
earlier to the peoples who had decided to 'modernize'
the planet.*

BRUNO LATOUR

Mother's singing to us now in a loud soft voice,
"Put your ear to the air and ground and sea."

Mother's singing in the brush, "You are me, You are me.
    You are me."

Mother's shedding her veils across the Earth.

Mother's starting her sentences with the word "unless."

Mother's wearing a tattered dress.

Mother's running a temperature.

Mother's echoing on the porch of our ears,
"The small rain down can rain."

Mother's weeping sour tears.

Mother's howling, "It's late, my dears."

Mother's chirping, "You're so many now. What to do?"

Mother's soloing in the overstory,
"Love's for nothing if you can't save me."
Mother's barking runes in the alley:

Nothing never turns to something when already there's far
    too much.
Wonder lives in the dirt like a worm.
Filaments and wings rhyme in the air.
Every creature is stranger and therefore far more beautiful
and original than anything anyone could ever imagine.

Mother's soughing in the breeze, "I'm waiting to hear."

Mother's writing time tables on the board of sky and then
    erasing them.

Mother's splashing Rorschachs in the clouds, each one of
    which translates,
"This is the age of necessity, my darlings, this very second."

Mother's yipping in her sleep, then saying nothing when
    she wakes.

Mother's growling, "You've swelled a progress to its tipping
    point."

Mother's twinkling from the stars to regard her from afar.

Mother's cawing, "You must do what seems impossible now,
but you've done it before."

Mother's peeping, "I'm miraculous, I'm miraculous, I'm
    miraculous…"

Mother's writing indelibly on water:
"If you don't lament the Pyrenean ibex, the passenger pigeon,
the Steller's sea cow, the western black rhinoceros, the dodo,
the quagga, the Pinta Island tortoise you'll have no heart at all
in the end to save yourselves."

Mother's cooing so sweetly, "You must imagine, imagine,
    imagine
in order to start."

Mother's hooting, "Science is not political! Not political!
    Not political!"

Mother's speaking in so many languages that are nonetheless
    one.

Mother's quacking and chirping and barking and purring
    and growling and braying and snorting and yodeling
    and keening and grunting and laughing and hissing and
    screaming and whispering.

Mother's speaking silently in every language: listen.

GRIEF IS THE RIVER
WITH A FOREIGN NAME

For the children who have died in Gaza

Grief is the river with a foreign name
that floods your heart, pulling you in
with a musical force you can't resist
for the song it plays inside the silence
of the things they left: the dress, the doll,
the drawings—transformers each on
the surface that runs through the country
of your heart, which is why we imagine
Earth as Heaven when we see their faces
in the surface of the river, memory's
mirror, and think they are real, although
we know they are floating to the sea
where they will join the others, although
we swear at the god of time who leads
us by the hand into the water and squeezes
our chests then holds us under for as long
as we can live without breathing while
the birds are singing and the clouds
are floating like letters that form their names
on the pages of sky that just keep turning.

SIC ET NON

"Yes," I said to taste the sweetness
that made me stutter.
"No," I lied to hide the truth
that was so bitter.

HOW TO DIET

Eat your hunger.
Put some sugar on it
and a little butter, too,
then eat it a 1,000 times
in all its various flavors
until you're so full
of emptiness, you could eat
a 1,000 more, but don't
because you've allowed yourself
a little morsel of celery instead
and a radish for dessert
to fatten your discipline,
a postprandial nibble that gives
you indigestion, but you chew it
anyway, remembering
the last cookie you had
four weeks ago as if it were now
and you're eating it again
in your head, which only angers
your stomach, who has captured you
and is holding you hostage
in a ramshackle cabin down a dirt
road somewhere you hope
will become famous some day
as the site where you outsmarted
it, your stomach, by simply keeping
your mouth shut, despite
the fact it's holding a gun
to your head with your finger

on the trigger, believing
that you just might pull it.
But I digress. Just eat it
with nothing on it.
It's good.
You'll see.

THE LACK

So I
am feckless I
admit,
for I
was born without
sufficient feck,
which is why
I take a supplement
of it,
along with all
my other pills
and stuff,
although it's never quite
enough.
So I
digress as a way
to curse
my dearth of feck,
as if
a prolegomenon or plot
could plug the drain
of my so leaky self,
and then
an afterward as well,
but no,
not yet.
I had a dream last night
in which
I was *enough.*

LATE WORK IN EARLY WINTER

I felled an ash yesterday that dropped
in the stream below the house with a thud
my neighbor heard from across his field where he
was digging postholes for a fence to keep
his cows from getting out again.
"Plenty of heat in that one," he said, startling me
from behind after walking over in the din
of my saw to see just what it was
I was doing so close to his land.
"Hello, Ed,"
I said in the quiet of my shut-off Stihl.
"Now all I have to do is pull it out
of the stream with my ATV."
"Yup" he said.
"Looks like that beetle got it
like all the others.
Sometimes I think I feel one
crawling up my shin."
He's ninety three
but can still fix almost anything on his farm
without any help, from backing his Massey
Ferguson out of a bog by chaining six foot
logs to its high rear wheels, then
creeping out, to fixing his ancient half-ton truck
with parts he's kept for fifty years because
he knew he'd need them even more down
the road than a brand new truck.
We talked
until it was almost dark and a star

came out in the late December sky.
A breeze blew in from the north
with a chill as we talked
some more about this and that,
I can't remember now.
"Be well," he said.
"You too," I replied,
and then, as he turned around after having
already turned around a couple of times
as if he were lost or had a few more things
to say but thought against it, he exclaimed,
"Will you look at that!"
"What?" I asked, looking up from the ash.
"That bank of fog heading this way
from across my field."
"Well, I'll be damned," I said
"It's a holy ghost the way it's floating there,
the way it just appeared from out of the blue
as a cloud and landed in your field like a parachute.
"What a sight!"
But he was gone, out of range,
and I alone again, stood weeping
there in the dark that was falling like a shroud,
as if I were the king of these parts in my crepuscular
gown with the sound of a voice I'd never heard
before calling to me, then not.

CREDO

I know more than I think I do.
Nothing is full of flowers.
The universe fits inside my head with room to spare.
This it is a literal place—a paradise of endings.
The sound of a falling tree goes unheard
in the light of a star that no longer burns.
Absence forms the shadow at the heart of light.
Time is at the mercy of thought.
I either live in this mercy or not
singing in the dark.

NOTES

Night Nurse

DSM stands for *Diagnostic Statistic Manual.*
The quoted lines in the poem are by the following
poets in the order they appear: Theodore Roethke,
John Clare, and William Shakespeare.

Abelard To Héloïse

Peter Abelard (12 February 1079 – 21 April 1142) was a me-
dieval French scholastic philosopher theologian, renowned
logician, and author of *Sic et Non (Yes and No).* His affair
with Héloïse d'Argenteuil has become legendary. Their
child was named Astrolabe.

The Book of Guests

The line *"terre nous aimait un peu je me souviens"* is from Rene
Char's poem "Évadné."